AF398894

Martin Fritzen

Esports Funding Guide

Author: Martin Fritzen
Editor-in-chief: Austin Redfern
Designer: kornerupdesign.dk

ISBN: 9788743009801

© 2019 Martin Fritzen

Publishing house: BoD – Copenhagen, Denmark
Production: BoD, Norderstedt, Germany

ESPORTS FUNDING GUIDE

How esports teams, organizations and sports clubs can create solid and profitable revenue streams and secure the operation and development of their esports activities.

"

Anyone who reads this will have a good understanding of the commercial mechanics in esports, and have a ton of actionable insights to implement right away. Great and informative book.

Jonas Gundersen, Chief Commercial Officer, NORTH A/S

Table of Contents

Introduction

Running an esports team or organization is hard and expensive. This book is written for esports teams, organizations and sports clubs working with esports. My mission is to provide a wide range of ideas and ammunition for potential revenue streams so you can develop and run profitable esports teams and organizations.

In 2015, I founded what is now one of the biggest esports organizations in Denmark with several teams and coaches, as well as hundreds of paying members and profitable revenue streams. In 2017, I was hired as the Esports Project Manager at Danish Gymnastics and Sports Associations (Danske Gymnastic- & Idrætsforeninger) (DGI). DGI is a sports association in Denmark that works to better the conditions for more than 6,500 member sports clubs and their more than 1.5 million members. My job is to lead a team of 14 people to develop esports activities in the 6,500 sports clubs around Denmark. For the last two years I have heard the same question over and over, "How can we make money to develop and run our esports team or organization?"

It is a fair question, as running an esports team is expensive. Depending on the size and ambition of the organization, you need money to pay for expenses such as salaries, apparel, media and content production, travel and accommodation, tournament fees, software, hardware, gear, sales and marketing. Additionally, you have to consider costs incurred from location, rent, utilities, internet, food and so on.

This book is a collection of successful experiences and strategies from over 100 esports clubs and organizations in Denmark. I have met and talked to over 50 esport and gaming industry leaders and brands like; Logitech, Microsoft, Red Bull, Razer and Intel, to understand, why and how they do esport partnerships.

This book is designed to provide you with an inspirational catalogue of ideas for you to create several profitable revenue streams, and thus, securely manage the operation and development of your esports team, organization or sports club.

The suggestions found in this guide are all based on my personal experiences working to help build grassroots esports in Denmark. All the advice that I give you has been tried and tested for esports organizations of all sizes, and I hope that it will help yours as well.

KEY TAKEAWAYS IN THIS GUIDE:

1. Develop strong teams and work with great people.
2. Build a unique mission statement based on your core values and vision.
3. Set simple and clear goals.
4. Plan 1, 2, and 3 years ahead.
5. Reduce your costs.
6. Understand why your organization is unique and how you can make a difference to partners.
7. Secure the revenue streams you will need to achieve your goals.
8. Understand how you make profit and how you scale your business.
9. Work hard and focus on partnership sales every day.
10. Be quality-oriented in everything you do.

11. Continuous development and learning.

Happy Reading,

Martin Fritzen

About the author

Martin knows all about success in esports. He founded what is now one of the biggest esports organizations in Denmark with several teams and coaches, as well as hundreds of paying members and profitable revenue streams. He is now leading esports activities at DGI - a sports association in Denmark that works to better the conditions for more than 6,500 member sports clubs and their more than 1.5 million members.

For the last few years, he has heard the same question over and over, "How can we make money to develop and run our esports team or organization?" This book is based on years of experience building and creating sustainable esports organizations with relevant partnerships, as well as several years of talking with esports organizations and companies sponsoring esports.

"I hope this book will inspire you to think outside the box so you can begin to build profitable revenue streams and achieve your esports dreams, just like so many others." – Martin Fritzen, 2019.

Chapter 1

Define your management team

Why do you need to define your management team? Investors, brands and partners invest in great teams, want to work with powerful and talented people, and most of all want to be a part of your company's success. Therefore, it is extremely important that you sit down with your management team and describe who you are, what you have done, why you are unique, and what you will accomplish together.

Brands and partners receive many proposals. You need to stand out and build trust so that when potential partners look at your esports organization, they will see that an investment in you makes sense. Too many esports startups focus on results. As an organization, you also need to communicate your personal values, skills and experiences. Define yourself and your management team by writing 7-10 lines about who you are, your education, your former successes, your skills, your likes and hobbies. For each managing partner, you will also need to list this information and explain why together, you form great management team. Why do you work well together? Why and how are you unique? Why should anyone invest in you and your team, instead of in the hundreds of other esports organizations?

COMPETENCIES IN THE MANAGEMENT TEAM
In a board or steering group in an esports organization, there are different people with different competencies, qualifications, experiences and education.

It makes sense that the tasks that are intended to achieve the goals are handled by people with competencies that fit it. Put another way, the person or persons who work with partnerships must like it, and be good at it.

One person can handle the dialogue with the municipality and local government. Applying for local grants and funds. One person can contact national and international grants and funds. One can work with fundraising from private companies and private funds and grants.

The work of searching for municipalities and foundations is typically about managing their project, their finances, their story (who they are, what they want and why they want to make a difference, etc.), and then applying for an amount to go to X purpose.

Working with partners can be a little more demanding, as you must meet often, present, negotiate, make agreements, cooperate on plans, and on the whole, execute.

It can easily be a special business group that works to contact foundations, municipalities and partners in order to effectively launch negotiations when a new effort and a new goal requires a new partner or economy.

Partnerships come in many sizes and formats. My experience is that the most important thing is that as an esports organization you have made it clear what you want to achieve with the partnership and why. Can you explain why you have just approached this partner and what you want to achieve? Can relevant partners can see themselves in the idea, and can you explain what's in it for the partner? If so, you are close to success.

Partners also have different goals, just like the sports clubs and organizations. Some want to support the local organization with time, money, equipment or services. Some want publicity and exposure/visibility. Some want activities, content, articles, videos and events. Some want positive press or CSR and some want something completely different.

Therefore, it is crucial that you as an organization find out what your partner wants. Ask the question: "Let's go forward 12 months and you are, as a partner, really happy about the partnership with our organization. Tell me what has happened. What have we done in the past 12 months that have made you happy?"

The answer to this will tell you what your potential partner is looking for and what goals the partner has. It is not useful, for example, to offer a logo on a website and a player's shirt, unless it is interesting for the partner. Always be open-minded and curious about what goals the partner isn't interested in and see if you can meet each other halfway.

My experience is that many partners want to enter esports and that the partners want to make a difference. Partners may not like to - passively - send thousands of euros to an organization where you do not know what the money is going to, but are interested in meaningful partnerships. Ones where you can see that the money and the commitment are making a difference for exactly the target audience and the organization you work with.

Define the organization and your goals

Before we start looking at money and partnerships in esports we need to start with the basics. Every esports organization must describe its mission, two V´s (vision and values), and goals. An organization's mission, vision and values set the direction of the organization. These may sound like things that only large companies need (or have the time to do) but you will quickly find that without direction, you will quickly get lost. These are essential, especially in the constantly changing environment of esports and gaming. In this chapter, I will show you how to define the DNA of your esports team through the mission, vision, as well as core values and goals.

When done right, these statements and lists will all tie into each other. The trick is understanding how each component provides value alone and then finding a way to thread them together. Make sense? Hopefully this will help…

❯ MISSION STATEMENT:
The mission statement states what your esports organization actually does. It should be short and easy to remember. A lot of organizations get this wrong and end up using big fancy words that don't really mean anything. Your mission statement should also be specific enough that people understand what you do and how it may differ from other teams and organizations. For example:

- The Chicago Bulls organization is a sports entertainment company dedicated to winning NBA Championships, growing new basketball fans, and providing superior entertainment, value and service.
  Source: https://on.nba.com/2vX9WAA

For esports it could be something about challenging the status quo, creating fantastic moments for esports fans, developing the greatest esports athletes, etc. You have to develop the mission statement for your organization based on who you are, what you want to do and with whom.

- More than just a team, Fnatic's mission to bring eSports into every household. Headquartered in London, the Fnatic operation spans across San Francisco, Berlin, Belgrade and Kuala Lumpur. From designing hardware gear and apparel to launching community experiences, we at Fnatic are dedicated to building the first globally recognized lifestyle brand to emerge from the world of eSports– and continuing to entertain new audiences far and wide.
  Source: https://bit.ly/2YsuNYZ

- Ninjas in Pyjamas´s mission is: strive to give our followers and our community the ultimate fan experience, whether it be through the highest level of esports, content creation, fan engagement, or merchandising. We want those who follow us to take part in our legacy and the history we are making; to be inspired by the Ninjas In Pyjamas and the NiP Standard in their everyday life.
  Source: https://bit.ly/2VZvKdG

❯ VISION STATEMENT:
This is what your company aspires to be which can be quite different from what your company is actually doing (your mission statement). When done right, your vision statement can and should help drive decisions and goals in your company. Here are some examples of some good vision statements:

- The Green Bay Packers' (NFL team) vision is to become and remain the standard of excellence against which all other organizations in professional sports are measured.
  Source: https://bit.ly/2E6XKBQ

- Fnatic's vision is to bring eSports into every household. Founded by Sam and Anne Mathews in 2004 in the early days of the professional video gaming industry, Fnatic has since helped shape the new world sport into a fast-growing phenomenon.

- At its core are Fnatic's talented professional gamers, who have won thousands of tournaments and inspired a community of tens of millions of fans.
  Source: https://bit.ly/2YsuNYZ

- Ninjas in Pyjamas aims to be the world's leading esports organization, both inside and outside the game. The term "NiP Standard" shall be synonymous with superior quality, professionalism and sound integrity.
  Source: https://bit.ly/2He9pRk

> **CORE VALUES:**

Core Values are what support your vision and shape the culture of your esports organization. They are your organization's principles, beliefs, and philosophy. Try limiting yourself to five core values. Once you get beyond five it's hard for your team to remember which are the most important.

Here is an example of the Ninjas in Pajamas' core values:

We are passionate about our brands, businesses, products, esports, and most importantly; the people who make up our fan base and communities around the world. Partnership and collaboration everywhere is essential. We create an environment where every Ninja is empowered to contribute and is recognized for their effort. We are committed to drive individual growth for our players, teams and employees, creating an inclusive culture where they all can develop and enhance their performance. We act with integrity and high ethics in all of our relationships. We strive for the respect and protection of fundamental human rights.
Source: https://bit.ly/2VZvKdG

Here is an example of the Orlando Magic's (NBA team) core values:

COMMUNITY • We are committed to investing in our community and strive to make our residents proud, knowing we represent them in all we do. We invest our time, talent and resources to positively impact the lives of our fans and our community. We help children, especially those most at risk, reach their full potential by investing in their future. We are dedicated to creating an inclusive environment in which our fans, community and employees feel welcome, valued and appreciated.

INNOVATION • We promote a culture of creative thinking and informed risk taking. We continuously challenge ourselves and ask "why" and what we can do to be the best. We drive change through collective creativity and foster an environment where employees are encouraged to take risks in an effort to achieve breakthrough results. We develop innovative ideas to achieve added value for our colleagues, partners, fans and the community.

LEGENDARY • We are committed to providing world-class service and entertainment to our customers by creating legendary moments. We are committed to winning with integrity. We do what is right, not just "what works." We hire and develop the best talent; employees that are passionate about delivering excellence.

TEAMWORK • is a key driver to our success on and off the court. We support teamwork through a culture of trust, respect and camaraderie. We practice selflessness on a daily basis and acknowledge that we are on the same team working towards one goal. We value multiple perspectives and diverse expertise. We foster a collaborative environment that allows for creativity in approach, ideas and suggestions for the greater good of the Orlando Magic. We are resilient and adhere to the values and vision of the organization, remaining positive through adversity while continuing to support one another.

Goals

Goals are important to serve as a compass so you know where and how to steer your boat. Without goals, your boat (or team) will set sail with no direction and with no goals to reach.

A lot of organizations are adopting Google's Objectives and Key Results (OKRs) methodology to set goals. I find this method helpful and have used it in my own work.

Objectives: The process begins by setting high-level objectives. Set a few goals, two, maybe three, for your esports organization. Separate them by department, team, or game. The idea is that every player, team, manager, and volunteer knows which goals they are working toward in order to know when and how successful they are.

Ideally, your objectives should align with your vision statement. While objectives are high level, they shouldn't be too vague. For example, avoid saying, "Have the best team ever" or, "Create a better website." Here are some good examples:

- Add a social media manager to our team
- Open our headquarters at X location
- Increase monthly recurring revenue (MRR) by 30%

Key Results: Key results are the other half of your OKRs. These are the tactics you engage in to meet your objectives. <u>They need to be measurable</u> so you know if and when you have achieved your goal/objective. Do not write too many, three or four should be good enough. Here are some examples of key results that would be connected to the first objective, "Add a social media manager to our team."

- Attend one hiring fair this quarter
- Create one blog post about hiring
- Use LinkedIn to reach out to five potential candidates

You will want your OKRs to be transparent. This may feel odd if it is your first time using OKRs, but this is where their strength lies. Everyone will be on the same page and understand what each other is working on and more importantly, why they are doing it. It also <u>helps you to align your goals</u> with your core values and your vision statement.

One final word of advice. During the strategic planning phase, make sure to include a diverse group of employees in the process. In other words, don't limit these planning sessions to just your executive team. When different levels of employees are involved in this process, they see the workplace as "theirs" as opposed to it belonging to management. It's a win-win for everyone.

All in all, if this is too technical or overwhelming, think of goals this way:

> You are a person, you want to go sailing. You go to the harbor, and jump on a boat. Unless you set a goal, you will just be sailing around, not going anywhere; at worst, you will crash and have to swim back to land. Goals will help you and your organization move towards finding success and creating a profitable business.
> Source: https://bit.ly/2Vm9t5k

Create the story of your esports organization

You'll find Nike's mission statement on their website under the about section. It says, "Bring inspiration and innovation to every athlete in the world." Source: https://swoo.sh/2xwpPN5

Behind that mission statement, Nike has created a story, vision, goals, and core values that all tie into each other in the form of their mission statement.

Having a story to support your esports organization is important. Your story is unique and will separate you from other esports organizations. It will make your organization stand out and it makes it easier for brands, partners, players and employees to connect with your organization and understand where you come from and where you want to go. While some think that business deals are all business, I believe that there are emotions involved and you must recognize the power in them.

Build your unique story by answering the questions below and find someone good with words to help you create a compelling, emotional story to which others can easily connect.

❯ WHY DO YOU DO IT?
Describe and know your why. Your why is critical in order to get buy-in from those around you. It demonstrates your motivation and makes it easier for people to get involved with your efforts and contribute with the same kind of passion and interest.

Most start with the what and the how, but I think that's the wrong approach. You must start by defining your why.

❭ WHO ARE YOU?

Start by jotting down some notes to describe your organization.
Why are you unique? Who is on the leadership team, who is on the
management team, what is your story, education, experience, where
are you located, etc.?

❭ WHY IS YOUR ORGANIZATION UNIQUE?

Describe why you are unique. Can you do something special, do you
work with specific or new audiences, or have you developed special
services that others do not offer? Do you have experience or an
education that differentiates you? Do you have a special story or new
and different skills and qualifications in your organization?

❭ WHAT IS YOUR VISION?

Will you make a difference worldwide? Do you want to make a
difference in the local community? Would you like to create a sense of
community for children with challenges at home or at school? Are you
interested in building an organization for the masses or rather for an
elite group? What do you and your team want?

❭ WHAT ARE YOUR DREAMS FOR THE ESPORTS ORGANIZATION?

Write down your dreams -- your innermost, wildest dreams and
desires for the organization. For example:

- Esports becomes as recognized and respected as football.
- Your organization grows to X size.
- Help X number of kids each year.
- Become a world champion.

Think big and be honest with yourself!

❭ WHAT WILL YOU ACHIEVE AND WHEN?

Get more detailed and explain your goals and deadlines for your
dreams. What will you achieve, how, when and with whom?

Want to win something? Write down the specific tournament or prize.
Should the organization have more members or develop new offers?

Find an exact number that you will aim for. What goals do you have as an organization? Make a list of your goals with realistic timelines.

❯ WHO CONTRIBUTES AND WITH WHAT?

What has your organization or management team contributed to the project? Time, money, materials, network, staff, volunteers, experience or something else? Who is involved and will contribute to achieve your goals?

Create an overview of your team. Who will be involved in each effort and who will take ownership of what?

❯ WHAT HAVE YOU DONE SO FAR?

Write down how you work, how often you meet with the management team and what you have done so far. Are there others around the organization that are also dedicated and invest time and resources in the project? Make sure to celebrate your progress so far even if it is just completing the first few steps to understand your DNA.

Case Study: Apple and their why

In order to better understand why I believe in starting with the *why*. Take a look at Apple. Apple's why is at the heart of their marketing and the driving force behind their business. To help illustrate this point, imagine if Apple started backwards and made a marketing message that started with *what*, their product.

What does Apple do? They make good computers that are user-friendly, beautifully designed and easy to use. Now think about that pitch, would you buy that computer? Probably not. Lots of companies make good computers that are user-friendly and have great design - it's not unique and it's not why we buy Apple products.

Apple's pitch is more like the following, *"With everything we do, we aim to challenge the status quo. We aim to think differently. Our products are user-friendly, beautifully designed, and easy to use. We just happen to make great computers. Want to buy one?"*.
Source: https://bit.ly/2QOTT48

Apple's pitch helps the buyer better identify with their feelings and their why - to challenge the status quo and the idea of thinking differently. It may well be that we do not challenge the status quo on a daily basis, it may also be that we do not always think differently, but we are willing to buy more expensive computers and phones that give us that feeling. This allows us to show the outside world that we are progressive and think outside the box, something that Apple represents (even if we don´t). This is key! Most partnerships are based on network, relationships, feelings and intuition.

The same goes for your esports organization. Tell others your why and they will follow you. What is your why? What is your motivation? Winning, hosting events, being an organization, or having 22,000 likes on social media is not interesting alone. You need a great story to back up the numbers. Decisions are both emotional and logical.

So make your story emotional and connect to your audience on a deeper level.

What is interesting is your team, your inner motivation and your ability to get things done. Consider the following:

- As a player, it may be that you want to change the classic stereotype of a gamer with pizza and soft drinks. This is an idea that others can buy into.
- As a team you may want to rethink your esports teams and include more women or promote anti-bullying - something others can buy into.
- As an event organizer, it may be that you will make an effort toward more inclusion and cooperate with organizations that advocate for persons with disabilities.
- As an organization, you may want to promote integration and collaborate with local asylum centers, job centers or even try to differentiate yourself by creating the most amazing moments in sports, ever.
- As an esports club, you may want to create the best players and teams and win masters and championships. You can team up with a strong sports club, utilizing the club's talent management systems and performance models to gain momentum and create the best results.

When you have found the answers to the questions above, have a clear idea of who you are, what you want, and why you are unique … then what? You know your goals, your inner motivation and your why.

This is your story and your DNA that partners, fans, players, coaches, funds and grants will want to be a part of and buy into.

Find that friend, or person in your network, who can help you write this into a compelling, emotional story that others can easily connect with. Put this story on your website, in your presentations, on your social media and have fans, partners, players - everyone - connect with it.

Take the HFX Wanderers FC, a team playing in the Canadian Premier League, founded in 2018. Their club and team are new founded in 2018. Nevertheless, they have a compelling and strong brand, with a great story to tell about the people and heart of Nova Scotia. You don't need hundreds of years to build a great brand or story, you just need to be creative, honest, and express your why.
Source: https://bit.ly/2LOCI6G

OUR HARBOUR, OUR HOME, OUR SOUL
Nova Scotians have heart. The evidence is everywhere. You hear it in the laughter, you feel it in the music. And the veins that pump life to every corner of the province originate from the same place; Halifax Harbour.

Communities grew on either shore nourished by the beating tide. Despite suffering unimaginable damage, it healed to become the main entry point for new Canadians. It's where you unloaded your bounty, and then celebrated after.

The Harbour is like Nova Scotians themselves...welcoming, even in the worst storm. It's also evolving. A rich history can sometimes be an anchor holding a city back. Not in today's Halifax. The wind is right, the sail is up...and there's something big on the horizon.

Young-old, male-female, Nova Scotian-newcomer; they'll all be invited. And they'll sing those hearts out. The harbour has inspired the club. The club motto Ar Cala, Ar Dachaigh, Ar n-Anam means: "Our Harbour, Our Home, Our Soul" in Gaelic.

Financing

How much money do you need, by when and for what? In order to figure this out, you'll need to start by setting some financial goals, initiatives, and timelines.

❯ SETTING FINANCIAL GOALS

Now that you have identified who you are and what your purpose is as an organization, you can move your attention to your goals and efforts. Start by describing your financial goals and then the tasks and efforts that will allow you to achieve them.

❯ GOALS

Setting goals helps you understand where you want to go and on what timeline. This helps you "steer your boat" and helps you specify and allocate budgets.

Your financial goals must align with your vision and mission. This is central to attracting partners. For example, if you want to build an organization that focuses on local social inclusion and then you suddenly stop working in that direction and start prioritizing elite Counter-Strike teams, you will lose your credibility and the trust you have built with your partners.

An example of a goal is, "We will open an esports organization and have 5 coaches and 50 paying members (players) before X date (6 months from today)."

❯ INITIATIVES

What tasks and initiatives are missing in order for you to achieve your financial goals? Creating a plan will be really helpful, even if you end up deviating from your original timeline or tasks. You may want to consider the following as inspiration for initiatives:

- A management team for the esports project
- Esports coaches
- Training and match concepts
- The games for which you offer training and matches (and how often)
- A target audience for the organization
- Facilities for training and matches
- Equipment -- can you borrow or buy esports equipment or build your own esports room/facilities? Or should players bring their own equipment or play online?
- Budget and finances
- Cooperation with parents and families
- Your stance on game ratings (PEGI/ESRB) and ethics
- Volunteer management and rewards
- Communication and initiatives towards anti-bullying, health, physical activity, performance models, etc.

> INTERNAL AND EXTERNAL INITIATIVES

You will have goals and initiatives that you can manage within your esports organization. For example, developing an exciting concept around training and matches. We call these "initiatives that require internal efforts."

You will also have goals and initiatives that you cannot immediately manage within a team. It could be about finding facilities, purchasing equipment, special events, boot camps, travel for tournaments, insurance etc. We call these initiatives that require cooperation from external partners "initiatives that require external efforts."

For many esports organizations, it will typically be the initiatives that require external efforts where relevant partners can come into play.

> AN EXAMPLE

It's helpful to see your goals and initiatives as two separate concepts. See the example below, and try separating your goals and initiatives into the two following categories:

IDEA OR GOAL

Create an esports organization where kids in the community between 8-14 years old can practice and play computer games. At the same time, we will create a safe, social space for board games, doing homework, becoming a part of the community and making new friends.

AIM OR INITIATIVE

To offer activities on our own premises three times a week and have 10 working esports stations in the room by X date.

IDEA OR GOAL

To have an esports organization with a Counter-Strike team ranked among the Top 100 in the world in 12 months.

AIM OR INITIATIVE

To offer an organization training, matches, and tournaments for five players and a coach (and win X% of every game played) before X date.

BUDGET

You are going to need to make a budget of all your expected expenses and income. The biggest mistake esports organizations make is forgetting to plan. Having financial plans for the next year, two years and even three years, helps your organization and demonstrates to your community that you've got things under control.

Consider the following categories when building your budget:

> FACILITIES

If you do not have access to rooms that can easily be transformed into an esports room / arena / center, talk to the local municipality to see if they have some available to lease. Alternatively, talk to other nearby sports clubs, schools, libraries, businesses, or youth clubs and find out if they have rooms that can be borrowed or made available.

❯ TABLES AND CHAIRS

Initially, common tables and chairs are a fine solution. The organization/sports club may also have some you can borrow but another good alternative is IKEA, where you can find tables/chairs for a reasonable price.

❯ INTERNET

Depending on the room you use, you may need to have internet installed. Prices and internet connections can differ significantly but as a starting point, you should have approximately 5 MB per active user. Thus, if you have 10 stations, you'll need a minimum of 50 MB. Internet for esports should always be wired and not Wi-Fi.

❯ INSURANCE

Call and speak with the organization´s insurance and security company. Esports equipment requires a new evaluation of your insurance and in some cases securing the esports room requires installing new security measures and alarms.

❯ SALARIES

Depending on your team and/or organization, you might need to hire people and pay them a salary. Some passionate people will join you as volunteers because you have a great project or a great vision and they share your values. Others, you'll need to pay. Always negotiate salaries, but be fair and reasonable.

❯ CLOTHING

Will you require team clothing, tournament jerseys, hoodies, travel clothing, t-shirts, etc.? Many teams, as in other sports, like to dress alike in order to demonstrate unity.

❯ MEDIA & CONTENT PRODUCTION

Will you pay for photography, video production, writing, infographics, memes, podcasts, streaming and casting? Perhaps you can find volunteers or parents to help with certain elements.

❯ TRAVEL AND ACCOMMODATION

How will you pay for team travel to events, meetings and tournaments?

❯ TOURNAMENT FEES

Paying for participation in tournaments. Consider how many tournaments you will want to participate in each year, and how many players will compete.

❯ SOFTWARE, HARDWARE AND GEAR

Will you have your own facilities/esports center or will you practice and play online? Your organization and players will need hardware, software and gear to participate. Consider the following: PCs, monitors, keyboards, mice, programs, etc.

You'll benefit from developing a relationship with your local IT business. Try inviting them for coffee and pitch the idea that you want to become partners. They are likely well connected in the industry and could be a good resource both for technical and professional reasons.

Be aware that it is your needs that indicate the price for the gear and equipment. The games you want to offer and your use case (training, events, tournaments, etc.) create the framework for which computers are needed and thus the price you have to pay.

❯ SALES AND MARKETING

You need to allocate budget to sales and marketing expenses such as the following: meetings, campaigns, software, PR, and advertising activities.

❯ SUMMARY

List all of your expected expenses and create a budget for the goals and initiatives you are looking to accomplish. You can make approximations of course but remember that the budget will be unique based on your individual situation.

Now that you have an overview of your expenses and the goal for your esports organization, you can really start working on finding relevant partners and creating revenue streams.

Chapter 4

Defining your services and products

What can you offer a new partner?

❯ SHOW YOUR BRAND IDENTITY
It's true that you can't judge a book by its cover, but it's also true that books are often recognized by their cover. Whether you are dealing with a small team, or international competition, you cannot introduce yourself with an inaccurate image. Invest your time and resources on a logo design and a visual identity that fits your DNA.

❯ CREATE DIFFERENT LEVELS OR PACKAGES OF PARTNERSHIPS
Remember, looking for a partner has nothing to do with asking for money. When dealing with partnerships, it is necessary to have a clear budget so that you can split it into partnership packages. These packages will be able to tell you, and your partners, that you have a well thought out pan. Your potential partners will understand why you need X amount of money to reach your goals for the next three years.

You can create different levels and packages and sell them to different kinds of partners in order to reach your goals. Obviously, a high-profile partnership will pay more and will consequently receive more marketing benefits from you. At the same time, partners that provide less support (either financially or in services) must be aware that they will receive less advertising from you.

Chapter 5

Creating your sales & marketing deck

❯ HOW TO CREATE PARTNERSHIP MATERIAL
Be simple and intelligent when you create the presentation of your esports organization, the marketing products and services, as well as the partnerships that you offer potential partners.

Your presentation could have:

❯ A COVER PAGE
The first slide of any presentation should be a creative and powerful cover page that you can use to introduce the presentation either at a meeting of a skype call. It will look great, and it will give you time to present yourself and your management team. Include a picture that appropriately communicates your vision, mission statement and values.

❯ ABOUT YOUR MANAGEMENT TEAM
This is the slide where you present yourself and your management team. Use great pictures here, while including just a bit of text. You do not want people to "sit and read" your slides, you want them to look at pictures, feel engaged and most importantly to listen to you. Make your management team look good and communicate brilliance and trust.

❯ ABOUT YOUR ESPORTS ORGANIZATION
This is the slide where you tell the story of your organization. Who are you, what do you do, where do you want to go, why should we believe you will succeed and how are you unique? Explain what you do and how you do it. What kind of teams, players, influencers or streamers do you work with?

> ACHIEVEMENTS
List the esports achievements your players and teams have achieved.

> GOALS
List the esports goals you are working to accomplish.

> TIMELINE
Include a timeline for your organization explaining how your
organization and leadership has developed while focusing on stability
and growth.

Show your products and how you can activate your community and
bring value to partners:

> LOCAL PARTNER ACTIVATION
(events, tournaments, viewing parties, collegiate esports, local social
media, local website, local venue brand placement, local player
or influencer marketing, event merchandise giveaways, as well as
whatever you can offer a partner locally).

> GLOBAL PARTNER ACTIVATIONS
(Live stream placements, global social media, global website, chat
bot messaging and links, sponsored video content, giveaways, online
tournement partnerships, endorsements, quotes, as well as whatever
you have to offer a partner globally).

> SOCIAL MEDIA ANALYTICS
Show the data from your social media per channel (followers,
engagement, reach and other KPIs relevant to your organization and
your channels. KPIs vary from channel to channel so make sure you
only use KPIs that brings value to the partner. You can use cavea.
io to collect and visualize all of your organizatin´s social media and
streaming analytics.

❯ WHAT ARE YOU LOOKING FOR?
Peripherals that will make your players better?
Monetary partnerships and activation? Other?

❯ AUDIENCE
Who can a partner reach when working with you? Which audience
can you present to potential partners? Gamers, boys, girls, men,
women, age, cities, countries, passions, etc.? Make sure you
understand which audience and target groups partners can connect
with by partnering with you. You can use cavea.io to understand your
audiences across all your social media & streaming channels.

❯ CONTENT
Make sure that you are coming up with specific initiatives that are
focused on delivering results and solving the partners' problem(s).
Really creative initiatives that don't achieve the intended purpose are
a waste of everyone's time. For example: if a partner is looking for
great, creative content for activating their brand and gaining reach,
you can create and promote videos like this: https://bit.ly/2FwdPCo.
If the partner is looking for sales depending on the size of your business,
you can offer collaborations like this: https://bit.ly/2HQT0mw.

❯ CASE STUDIES
If you can, show a case where one of your partners shares the story
about why they are your partner, what kind of partnership this is, and
what value they gain from the partnership.

Show logo placements from shirts, streams, social media, websites
and more, so partners can imagine what a partnership with your
organization looks like.

Show media activations, if you have any video content, podcasts,
graphics, streams or anything, where you have worked with a partner,
put that in, to visualize how it can be.

If possible, show event activations. How have you worked with partners at events? Do you have any pictures or videos that will make the partner look good?

Show how you have advertised a partner on live streams. How it looked, how many viewers tuned in, as well as the engagement.

All in all: in the presentation, you want to visualize how the potential partner will look amazing when working with your esports organization. Also, it is very important to create case studies and have pictures and video content whenever you do a partnership so you can continue to add valuable content to your case study portfolio.

Case studies will help potential partners feel safe and visualize themselves achieving success when working with you and your esports organization.

❯ MEASUREMENT
Put in (anonymous) data from previous partnerships to show how you measure partnerships. Include data such as "clicks", "viewers", "engagement", "visitors", "sales" – or whatever KPI you've decided to use. This data will show that you know what you are doing and will build trust, so the partner feels that you understand that data-based ROI measurement is important. Use cavea.io, Google Analytics and other services, to meassure and visualize data.

❯ BUSINESS OPPORTUNITY
Make sure that you sum up the business opportunity for the partner. Present the solutions, products and services that fit the partner's needs that you discovered during the previous phone call or previous meetings. What is the price to pay and what do you estimate the ROI will be?

> PARTNER MANAGEMENT

Align expectations and agree on KPIs that will define the success of
the partnership with the partner. Explain how you will follow up and
report on agreed KPIs. Understand how you can keep the partner
happy. Ask the question: "When we look 12 months ahead, and
you are extremely happy with the partnership – what did we do
together?". That will make the partner reflect on "What is success
to me?", and he or she will give you all the key ingredients for you to
achieve that success in the partnership.

> CONTACT DETAILS

Yes, sometimes people build presentations and forget to include
names, roles and contact details. Remember to include such
information so the partner can always have it on record.
Esports organization presentation example Pittsburg Knights
https://bit.ly/2BYFglY

Credits to: Pittsburg Knights. Fueled by the drive of talented
individuals, the Knights represent the concentrated ambition to
achieve one goal: TO BUILD THE IDEAL ESPORTS TEAM FOR MANY
YEARS TO COME. Under the guidance and leadership of veterans
within the esports and tech industries, the Knights represent the
paragons of esports. Our core mission is to take the best practices
from traditional sports and apply them to esports. Pittsburgh is the
City of Champions; it has a long history of strong sports franchises
and passionate fans. We want to take up that mantle and continue
the legacy of the city we grew up in. We didn't set out to build a
team, we wanted to build a legacy.

Chapter 6

Presales

Before you start contacting any potential partners, make sure that you have a strong suite of services and products you can sell to a partner and make sure your presentation is strong and properly sells your brand. We just went over this, I am sure you did great!

Now it is time for you to conduct research. What kind of partners will fit your esports organization, your values, your vision and your activities? Look for potential partners whose values match yours. When you choose a partner, you also have to love their products and services. You have to feel positive about their brand so you can endorse them where and when you have the opportunity. It's also important to keep in mind the state of your organization when conducting research. Is your organization new and looking to get started? Do you operate locally from a great esports venue? Are you an older, stronger esports organization, looking to expand your partner network?

Who are you, and what are you looking for – it is unique to each organization. Therefore, it is even more important that you are completely clear about: are you looking for local, regional, national or international partners? Which products and services do you believe you can sell to which partners? Understand how much revenue you need generated per month and year.

Start your research, look for partners by looking at existing esports or traditional sport organizations. Find which organizations you resemble the most and find out who they partner with. You may want to start by contacting similar partners. Also, don't hesitate to look locally, are there any local businesses that could be your next partner?

Research potential partners and put them into a CRM system like HubSpot. Use social media, local media, Google, LinkedIn as well as your contacts to find the right person and how you can contact them. In other words, who is the person that can sign a partnership contract with you? That is the person you want in the system, and the person you want to hunt.

You can make simple discovery calls to potential partners to understand if X person is the right person to talk with in terms of partnerships. Understand the potential partner's business. What do they do and how do they make money? What are they struggling to accomplish? Always Google a potential partner to see if there are any interesting facts about them in the media. You can then use this information to put into the CRM system to make your relationship with them stronger.

When entering a potential partner in your CRM system you can add info about who they are sponsoring right now and why you find this partner important, and how you can envision working together to build a strong partnership.

Make sure you think about industry exclusivity. Most partners like to be the only one in their "category".

❯ HERE ARE SOME OF THE CATEGORIES FOR
   WHICH YOU MIGHT LOOK FOR A PARTNER:

- Peripherals: keyboard, mice, mousepads
- Audio: headset, headphones, speakers
- System: PCs, consoles and laptops
- Transport, travel & accommodation
- Mobile phones and tablets
- Food & Beverage
- PR and media
- Betting
- Chairs
- Clothing
- Merchandise

Category exclusiveness makes the partnership stronger and is a good way to focus all your efforts into one partner per category.

Before you put any potential partner into your CRM system, make sure you feel that when you close this partnership, you will be happy! Not only that, your fans and audience will be happy and excited about the new partnership and new brand joining your ranks. After all, your fans and audience are the ones following your players, watching your streams, and buying your merchandise. They are the ones that you ultimately want to please.

Always dedicate a person to presale who loves research and discovery and who is detail orientated. You need as much relevant data in your CRM system as possible in as good quality as possible so that the sales executive can be as effective and efficient as possible.

Chapter 7

Sales

Now you have a CRM system full of interesting and relevant potential partners to call and with whom you can schedule meetings. I have spent over 20 years in sales and business development, allow me to share some of my best experiences with you so you can be as successful as possible at selling partnerships.

❯ FEEL HAPPY

Before you do anything, you should feel happy. If cold calling and sales does not make you happy, find someone else to do it. Put on some great music, stand up, shadow box. Do what you can to build energy in order to feel strong, energetic and powerful.

❯ BE ORGANIZED

Open the CRM system and start to work from a-z. Look up the first lead, read about it, what did the pre-salesperson put in. Write down your own notes when talking to anyone at the partner company, make sure you write down names, roles and details, of the people with whom you speak to keep the CRM properly updated. Make sure to include some "next steps" on how to proceed with this partner; what are we doing next and who is responsible for doing that? Make sure to contact everyone on your list and do not let any partner feel left out.

❯ BE PREPARED

Before calling anyone, make sure you look up their website, research the decision maker, connect with decision maker on LinkedIn, and read the notes from the CRM system. Please, please, make sure you are 100% clear about: Why are you calling this particular partner and not anyone else? What is your goal with the call? How can you see the partner work with your esports organization? How can you bring business or results to this particular partner?

❯ BE CONFIDENT

I know you have done all of the work I have inspired you to do in this book, so I know that you know your self and your management team well. You know your esports organization, who you are, what you do, where you want to go, how to get there and why you are unique. You can feel safe, confident and proud because you have a strong case and you bring value to this partner. All you need is the partner to pick up the phone and talk to you, right? Be confident. Feel proud.

❯ HAVE A CLEAR GOAL

I have always made a clear goal with my call. I am calling to ask for a meeting, I would like to spend 20 minutes with you so I can understand what you do and why you are doing so well. I always ask for a meeting so that we have dedicated time to dive in deeper in the conversation. Book that meeting. Face to face or skype will do.

❯ BE RELEVANT

Be relevant, when you contact people. Never, as in never, use copy pasted content. Always contact people or businesses because you have an individual and specific plan and idea with that specific contact or message. I have spent years talking to brands and partners in sports and esports, and each day they get so many generic, standard messages: "Do you want to sponsor my blah blah". Do not do that, do not waste anyone's time with irrelevancy. Be sharp, intelligent, relevant and be 100% clear about why you have chosen to contact this specific person or business. This will help you stand out from the rest and you show respect to the other person and you will get more responses.

❯ USE YOUR TOOLS

In sales, you can use email, social media, Skype, phone calls, face to face meetings and more. My advice will always be - you need to meet people. If not in person, then on a video call. Your persona, body language and tone of voice is so important for the relation with the other person, which is the foundation for the partnership in general. And in my humble opinion, if a person is not willing to talk to you or meet you then you might not want to do a partnership anyway. Use every tool you can to set up that meeting, and this is where you bring your a-game!

❯ BE OPEN AND CURIOUS

No matter where you are, and what you do, make sure you enter conversations with people. Ask questions such as: who are you, what do you do, for how long have you been doing that, what are you trying to accomplish, what is working great for you, what is a struggle right now? Ask open questions to get to know people at parties, networking events, birthdays, etc. Developing your network and nourishing your relationships, will bring you many sales during the years to come.

❯ CALLING

I always loved cold calling. Find the right person, call and wait for the person to answer and deliver the pitch. I want to understand who the person is and if he/she is the right decision maker or if I need to talk to someone else. With whom can I sign a partnership deal? Let´s book that meeting.

COLD CALLING SCRIPT EXAMPLE

I know, I know, there are so many different ways to do sales, but something like this has worked for me for 20 years, use it or design your own. Let´s go!

1) Get their attention by using their name. Start off my saying ”Hi, _____,” in a warm and welcoming tone, then proceed directly to Step 2. Notice I didn't say, ”Hi, _____, how are you today?” because it gives your prospect a chance to jump in and disrupt your flow. Cold calls are all about taking control in the beginning.

2) Identify yourself. ”My name is John with Starlight Esports” This is pretty straightforward — you need to tell them who you are.

3) Tell them why you're calling. "The reason I'm calling is to get some time on your calendar." Diving right in demonstrates that you're a professional. Save the small talk for your follow-up calls after you've already built the relationship.

4) Build a bridge. This statement connects the reason you're calling with why they should care. "I just noticed on your site that you're sponsoring Blue Nights Basketball team. Several companies sponsoring basketball teams are already working with Starlight Esports to reach new audiences and tap into digital marketing in a simple an easy way. They are also able to cut marketing spend and gain new business network."

5) Ask for what you want and shut up. "I thought the best place to start is to schedule a meeting to learn about your marketing strategies, sponsorships and goals. Do you have time Wednesday or Thursday afternoon around 10 a.m.?" Ultimately, our goal is to set meetings with prospects.

You have to:
- Understand why the company is sponsoring the traditional sports club?
- What does the company gain from that?
- What is this company trying to achieve?
- Is there a business opportunity between your esports organization and the prospect?
- Can your esports organization help the company to achieve that?
- Go for the meeting. Do not accept "Sending some info via email".

❯ FOLLOW-UP

Keep in mind that marketing managers, owners and investors are busy and it is possible that your proposal, even if interesting, is not be a priority. Agree on a better time to follow-up with those who seem interested but also, remind yourself that every "no" is also good news. You don't need to waste time on companies that are not interested.

❯ DON´T FALL FOR IT

Loads of sales calls ends with, "Send me your presentation and I will have a look". This is a common trick, don´t fall for it. Be honest, "Look, I know we can work together, I have a few ideas on how we can build a truly meaningful partnership that will pull in results for both of us. I really want to share these ideas with you, and that is why I'm asking for 20 minutes of your time. Sounds fair enough?". By being direct, you will project honesty and authenticity.

❯ AT THE MEETING

You have booked the meeting and you are ready to close the partnership. You have to be prepared, relevant and sharp at this meeting. Make sure that your presentation is ready, and tailor made to this meeting and to this potential partner. Make sure you understand the potential partners compelling event: why are they talking to you? What can you and your esports organization help them achieve? How can you be successful together?

I have always seen a sales meeting as a dance, first it can be awkward, and you dance in front of each other. At one point you get in sync and follow the same rhythm getting closer and closer. If you try to get to close to fast, the other part will move away like, "Hey there partner, that´s a bit to fast for me"... and you just start over. You can mess it up, but you can always just ask, "Right, remind me, what is it you like about our esports organization?". The question might seem crazy, but it is not. It will make the potential partner explain why they like you and why you are at this meeting, and not anyone else.

You list the needs the partner told you about: they want to reach X audience, they want to be visible to gamers in the local community, they want to support a talent oriented esports organization or what ever the compelling reason is, remind them of what they told you,

"You´ve told me that you need to do X, and that it is important to you so you can reach your goals for this year, is that correct?" ... "yes"... odds are, you will get acceptance.

You can continue on from there, "Based on all the info you gave me at this meeting, and that you want to achieve X, I would suggest we do x y z together, or I would suggest you pick this package. It will secure you a nice reach in the audience you need, and it will give you engagement from the audience and you will become part of the network program where you will meet other industry leaders in esports."

I suggest our gold package costing 15.000 EUR per year, we agree on one year and if you are pleased with the performance, re-negotiate after 10 months, sound fair enough?"

And then you leave the silence to the partner and the room. At one point he or she will say yes or no. The "no" is not a no. It is just a, "Hey there partner, you are a bit to fast for me". Then you just go back again asking, "Right, remind me, what is it you like about our esports organization? Why are we sitting here?".

Get it? It´s a dance and as long as you are polite, relevant, persistent and respectful, you will get the sales you need.

> ALWAYS
Always have one dedicated person working with partnership sales. Focus on volume and quality. If you contact 10 potential partners per day, you might close one sale per month. If you contact 100 potential partners per day, you might close 10 sales per month. Continue working with presales and sales in order to build a huge pipeline and a lot of sales activities to secure the revenue you need.

Partnership management

Now that you have closed some partnerships, you have to keep your partners happy. The general rule in partnership management or "customer success", is happiness. Keep your partners happy, and they will stay with you. If the partnership still makes sense of course. If the partnership is negative in anyway or takes up too many resources, you need to talk to each other to understand how you can improve it.

❯ SET CLEAR EXPECTATIONS
Depending on the partnership, you have to set clear expectations. How do you measure ROI and success of the partnership? Which KPIs should you report, how should you report them and how often?

Do you have to do weekly, monthly or quarterly updates? Who (with the partner) are you reporting to? Do they want meetings, calls or emails?

Setting clear goals and milestones for the partnership will make it so much easier for you to re-negotiate and document your success. Ask yourself the question, "So if I reach this goal / KPI, am I happy and do I feel that the partnership is beneficial? Am I ready to sign a deal for two or three years?".

❯ SEND OUT INVITES
You can host online or offline meetings or business events for your partners. Make sure you invite everyone, and include their names and make it personal. Also, if your teams are playing a great final or tournament that would be relevant for the partner to be part of, think of putting them on the guest list and make them feel great.

❯ GIVE MORE THAN EXPECTED
You can give your partners more than they expect. This could be handwritten cards on holidays, a personalized jersey or flowers and

a small box of candy. You can reach your goals and deliver more than the partner expects but doing something that shows that you have taken the time and thought of your partner will help build your relationship. Gestures such as these often come at a minimal cost and are always beneficial to both parties.

❯ BUILD A PARTNER PROGRAM
For some organizations, it makes sense to build a partner program where you offer events, services, meetings, networking, news and secrets to your partners. Partner programs are widely used in traditional sports and such programs are based on what kind of organization you run. Online, local, national, international – there are many ways to do it. What can you offer your partners that would benefit them?

❯ HIRE A PERSON
Have someone in charge of partner management or customer success. People who are great salespeople are necessarily not the best at creating detailed monthly ROI reports, following up, keeping a partner happy, receiving complaints, working around complex issues and finding new solutions so the partnership becomes successful.

Ideas to generate revenue

How to find profitable revenue streams for your esports team, organization or sports club.

LOOK LOCALLY FIRST.

Now you know your organization. You know where you want to go, why, how and when. You know how much money you need to accomplish your goals.

LET'S CREATE REVENUE.

Unless you are a millionaire, a former world champion, or the former CEO of Google, you want to begin with creating revenue streams. You can find such revenue streams from local, regional and even national companies, grants, funds and partners.

Remember, depending on what your goals are, your efforts and partner-opportunities will be different. If you want to build a local esports organization with a local esports center and offer exciting esports activities for your local community - the opportunity for partnerships will be found locally, maybe regionally.

If you are building an esports organization to reach national or international fans/audiences, the opportunity for partnerships will be regional, national and maybe even international.

It is always a good idea to look locally to start. This is where you have your network, and your relationships. This is where people know you, and where you have earned credit and respect.

Consider the following:

Do you know any local business owners that you can speak with about supporting your esports organization?
Next: What local companies are existing sponsors of existing sports & athletic clubs? Meet them and understand why they do what they do. See if your organization can help them with their goals.
Does the municipality or local government have funds or grants that support local activities for the esports team and/or the age range of kids etc.?
Are there any local funds, e.g. banks, LIONS, Rotary or other organizations that would be interested in supporting your cause and goals?
Are there any other funds or grants that can be used to support costs for the target audience of your esports organization?

It's important that you have an overview of the gap between what you can cover of the budget and what you need from partners. Make sure you are ready with specific numbers for any donations and contributions and are also able to show the results from the contributions.

Create revenue: ideas

1 ❖ FAN CLUB MEMBERSHIPS
Offer memberships to your organizations. People, parents, fans
will follow your organizations, cheer for you, and be part of them.
Creating a club for members, where you offer premium content,
streams, videos, tickets, merchandise or whatever you can develop
– will secure membership revenue for your organization.

Look at the soccer club F.C. Barcelona for example, they offer a club
for members for which they charge an annual fee:
Source: https://bit.ly/2LNWt9o

I know you are not F.C. Barcelona, just use the same model on a
smaller scale. 100 members paying 25 EUR per year, is still 2500 EUR
per year.
Paying members can receive a welcome package:

- Membership card personalized with photo
- Club statutes Badge
- Welcome letter
- Personalized certificate

These elements are not expensive, but will make a huge difference for
the member.

2 ❖ SUBSCRIPTION FEES
If you have a local esports organization with an esports center that
offers esports training and matches - you can offer subscriptions.
The price of a contingent in an esports organization may vary a lot and
often depends on where in the country your organization is housed
and of course also of what the members get for the price. The price
for the membership should reflect the benefits of membership and
before your organization sets the rate, it should define what the

members really get for their participation. If you have any doubts about what it should cost be a member of the organization, you can contact other sports clubs and learn from their expertise and experience.

Membership revenue naturally grows as the organization gets more members. To ensure additional membership revenue, it is a good idea to encourage coaches, leaders, parents and other interested parties to remain supporting members. Always make sure that each paying member "gets something back" and that it is an advantage for the individual to be member of the organization.

3 ⚐ EVENTS

Create online or local esports events. Get partners to pay for the infrastructure and prize pool, and charge teams for participating in the tournament/event. By doing so, your organization can make revenue on ticket sales, sales of food and beverages and potentially from new memberships. Think about the events that have the greatest potential to become a success and thoroughly investigate in advance what events and activities the target audience demands. Prepare well before the arrangement, make a budget and tightly manage costs to make a profit.

4 ⚐ RENT OUT ESPORTS FACILITIES

If your organization has local esports facilities, you can rent them out.

Schools, educational institutions, youth clubs, companies, local health, and mental health centers, are examples of some of the possible "customers" that your organization can contact and possibly rent your premises and facilities.

For example, schools and educational institutions can use the premises for teaching in esports and gaming as electives while social psychiatry and special schools can use the facilities for training concentration, learning and cooperation. Before the organization starts renting premises and facilities, it is a good idea to contact the municipality and examine how a rental income will affect any local government subsidies if applicable.

Other ways to secure income with your esports facilities is to host viewing parties, BlizzCon events, "Burger, drinks and ESL Masters" and so on. Another option is to contact every single hotel and conference centers within a 30 km. area and offer your esports activities as fun experiences to guests. Contact every business in the region to offer your esports facilities as fun collegiate activities or activities at a Christmas party or other general events.

5 ❖ MEDIA RIGHTS SALES
If your club/team is good enough, you can qualify for or be invited to a tournament, where you can benefit from a share of the media rights. This is typically only for professional teams.

6 ❖ MERCHANDISE SALES
If your team or club develops a fan base, you can start offering fun and engaging merchandise. Do this, develop it with your fans, and they will buy it. No matter how big or small the club is.

7 ❖ STREAMING
Open an account on Twitch and start streaming/broadcasting your trainings and matches. If you can find great casters/commentators, you can build a fan base and start earning money from fans by bringing them engaging, fun and quality content. You can also stream meetings, events, and festivals as well.

8 ❖ YOUTUBE
If you have a dedicated video crew, you can start by creating a YouTube account and documenting the creation of the esports club. Later, you can create and post unique, creative content that will give you a platform to show your viewers what your club is all about, and thus create an audience.

9 ⇶ SOCIAL MEDIA

Like YouTube, the same goes for Snapchat, Facebook, Twitter, Instagram or any other social media platform. It is an avenue to engage in a fun, positive, creative and respectful way with your fans, and to grow your audience; an audience you can convert into revenue through membership sales, merch-sales, ads, events, eBooks, signed posters, etc. Just be relevant and creative, give your target audience more than they expect, and only be on a platform if you use it. It is counter intuitive to be on Twitter and send two tweets per year.

10 ⇶ CROWDFUNDING

You have the opportunity to reach out to your community of fans and members to offer them a way of supporting your club/team, through crowdfunding. This can be organized through websites such as kickstarter.com where you can offer the fans merchandise, VIP services or other rewards in return for their support. You can also fundraise through monthly subscriptions with patreon.com where you can offer your patrons new content, videos, images, merch or other services, for their monthly support. Here is a guide:
https://bit.ly/2d7LUed

11 ⇶ PRIZE POOLS

Usually when an esports team or player wins money, the prize goes directly 100% to the player and team. Some teams split 10/90 or 30/70 with the organization or club.

12 ⇶ ADS

When your Twitch and YouTube channels have enough fans watching, you can use ads to generate revenue from the media.

13 ⇶ AFFILIATE PROGRAMS

If you can build a website, email newsletter and/or social media channels with a large following, you can begin to use affiliate marketing to promote affiliate campaigns via your media, earning provisions from every sale made through your channels. "Amazon Associates" could be a place to start.

14 ❖ DONATIONS

When you build an esports organization and offer your fans great content, great moments, and great experiences - some fans become ambassadors. The ambassadors will talk positively about your organization, promote your organization and they are most likely to offer donations to your organization, when you host different types of events. By adding a simple "Donate" option to your website and social media channels, you give your fans the opportunity to support the esports organization they love.

15 ❖ SIMPLE PARTNERSHIPS

Create a "Wall of founders", and offer every company or person, who pays a certain annual sum a spot on the wall. The "wall of founders", can be a real physical wall with plaques, or made as an online graphic. A lot of local sports clubs do this and offer "your name on the wall", for 100 euro/year for at least 3 years. Sell 30 partnership deals, and you have secured 3,000 euro/year in revenue from that wall. All you have to do is to send the partner a certificate as a PDF via email as reconnection.

You can find more inspiration here: https://bit.ly/2HjNirw

16 ❖ PARTNERSHIPS

Secure relevant partnerships with companies and brands. Sometimes you can land a partnership on a money-deal, where the partner will pay you monetarily. Sometimes the partnership will be about services. For example, the partner will give you 10x new headsets that you can give to your players, or offer to your fans, as prizes in social media competitions. Sometimes, you can work out individual partner deals, such as a supermarket chain that offers fresh fruit to your players while they are at tournaments.

If you are a smaller, local or semi-pro esports organization, I would still suggest you begin talking to your local businesses, offering them courses, knowledge and value around digital marketing. Most of local businesses have issues with being great at digital marketing. One way to provide value is to invite them to your organization and assist them with their digital marketing issues. By offering local business value, you build relationships. In turn, from these relationships, their interest in supporting your organization will grow.

Apart from that, I would most definitely map out 250 or 500 local and regional businesses, that could invest in one of your esports partner packages, and start cold calling to book meetings and close contracts.

TYPES OF PARTNERSHIPS

There are typically two types of partnerships: passive and active. It's important to know and understand the difference when approaching companies.

A.   THE PASSIVE PARTNERSHIP
The passive partnership is the traditional type of partnership in sports clubs. An example could be the local plumbing company that has a logo on the player's clothing or a sign on a computer or chair. They might support the club with 1,000 euro/year in return for advertising. It is an arrangement that is commonly used in the sports world where the partner achieves exposure, advertising and goodwill in return for the local sports organization receiving some financing.

B)   THE ACTIVE PARTNERSHIP
In this partnership, the company is an active participant. For example, your esports organization might make an esports tournament and their partner will set up a "Just Dance" game and some dancers from the local dance academy/school on the day. They will help create a great atmosphere, while the partner contributes financially or alternatively pays tournament fees. There is activity from both parties in the partnership and the partnership is about activities where both you and the partner contribute.

An active partnership could also be for the exchange of services. For example, a local advertising agency could contribute by making Facebook ads and writing articles for social media. They could also offer to pay for the advertising and in return have their logo on your club's shirts.

Another example of an active partnership is full partnership. We'll take the example of "NorBank." Let's assume they pay for all of the equipment for the esports organization and in return they get their NorBank logo on the shirts and website of your team. Additionally, you create some articles and videos when setting up the new NorBank esports hall, which they help finance. Together you create recurring NorBank esports tournaments on the premises. It creates goodwill, publicity and exposure for the partner and the organization grows. But most importantly, the partnership fits both the organization and NorBank's values and ideals: "supporting and developing the local community through good cultural, leisure and sports activities."

An active partnership could also be a company paying for a video or series of videos where the esports organization includes product placements or interacts with the brand in other ways. The brand or business gains brand awareness and reaches new audiences through the esports organization and esports organization gets money.

17 ⁂ EDUCATE OTHER PLAYERS

If your esports organization has its own esports facilities (room / building and computers), you can invite the local youth to visit your facilities and participate in esports education once a week. You or one of your players/coaches, can offer a 90-minute speaking session about a topic, and local players and gamers can buy a ticket for 10 EUR to join the session. This can be done online as well.

20 participants, paying 10 EUR will be 200 EUR per week. If you hold just 10 sessions per year, you will generate 2,000 EUR in yearly revenue from these sessions.

18 ⚐ EDUCATE PARENTS

Using the same model as above, you or someone in your organization,
can host a weekly session for parents to understand "their gamer
child".

19 ⚐ EDUCATE COMPANIES

In general, esports organizations are usually really great at using social
media, streaming and digital marketing to market themselves. Use
that knowledge, and sell on location or online courses to companies,
on "how to get great at digital marketing". This works great for local
companies, who are looking for inspiration in this field. This will also
be a great way to meet and talk to potential partners.

20 participants paying 40 EUR will be 800 EUR per week. If you
hold just 10 sessions per year, you will generate 8,000 EUR in yearly
revenue from these sessions.

20 ⚐ HELP OTHERS

Look around in your local community, there will be sports clubs,
schools, business or others, who are looking for help. Could be
help on a Christmas fair, help with a summer party, or help with
selling tickets to a lottery or an auction. Read local newspapers and
be proactive in contacting local fairs, parties and other initiatives,
usually it will be a way for you to earn money for your organization. If
there are 10 people in your organization, you can earn even more by
helping others out.

21 ⚐ LOCAL ESPORTS TOURNAMENTS

Hosting local esports tournaments can be a revenue stream. If you
or someone in your organization has the skills to host an esports
tournament, you can contact local schools, high schools, universities,
internet / gaming cafes, the local shopping center, libraries, tourist
centers, or local businesses and invite everyone to your event.

"New Jersey Spring EsportsCup. Team up with your friends and
compete to become the next New Jersey esports champion in games
like: Fortnite, League of Legends, DOTA2, CS:GO and more!"

The above is just a quick example of how you can pitch your event to your community.

Create a simple website and manage the tournament/teams/players via Battlefy or Tournament and charge each team an inscription fee of 10 EUR. Work with a local school, internet-cafe or other facility that can provide the computers/consoles you will need for the tournament and contact local business and invite them to join the tournament as a team of colleagues to compete against other business in the city.

As prices for 1st, 2nd and 3rd places, you can design and print free certificates. You can also work with a local trophy and medals-company, who might want to sponsor trophies and medals for the tournament. Ask the local shopping center if they would be willing to offer a gift certificate to the winner.

You and your organization can design the local tournament as you want, but in the end, you will host an esports tournament involving the whole local community that is financed through participant's fees. By doing this, you also show the local government, local businesses, hotels and conference centers that your organization can organize these types of tournaments and events - which might lead to more business for you.

If you stream this tournament, you can sell live partnerships for the streams. You can talk to local sports stores and invite them to do merchandise giveaways throughout the tournament.

You can of course offer local business to purchase advertisements to be displayed around the tournament facilities.

You can invite the local media to come to the event and invite them backstage to see what is going on! This is a great way to get free press coverage.

22 ❧ LOTTERY FUNDRAISING

Most countries have an opportunity for sports clubs and organizations to raise money with lottery sales. Sportsclublottery.com is one tool you can use. The basic idea is that your organization sells lottery tickets to your fans and local community, and through those sales, earns money for your organization. It is as simple as that. If there are 10 of you in your organization, selling 100 lottery tickets worth 5 euros each, you will generate 5,000 euros in revenue. Do this two times a year, and you will generate 10,000 euros in yearly revenue from lottery sales.

23 ❧ CONTENT CREATION

Being in gaming and esports, we usually have skills in creating videos, articles, pictures, podcasts, streaming channels and other great content because we have played around with creating content for many years. For some of us, it was because we wanted to become big on YouTube or Twitch, for others because we wanted to become a great content creator.

If you or someone in your organization has skills in creating content, it could be a way to earn money. Maybe you can help local business, as mentioned before in the "educate" idea. Maybe you can serve as an agency, creating content for businesses social media? Maybe you can produce profile-videos of local business, or help them understand how they can use Instagram, Snapchat, Facebook or other social channels? Maybe you can write SEO articles for local businesses?

Maybe you can collaborate work with local businesses. Let's say that a furniture store, needs new pictures and videos of their store. So you work with a local photographer - and together you create amazing photos, drone and in-store videos, you cut the videos and edit them, and in the end, you provide the furniture store with amazing new photos and videos - so they can promote their store.

You invite the photographer to the next business network event you host, so the photographer can meet new potential clients. Whenever you talk to businesses, keep in mind that if they need new photos or videos, you know a great photographer.

This way you help the furniture store. You help the photographer and you get paid from both the furniture store and the photographer for helping them out.

There are millions of ways to earn money from content creation: logo design, writing articles, graphic design, video, audio production, and animations. Creating collaborations, designing whole campaigns, working with streaming and social media. Imagine the local ice cream store, broadcasting live from their Facebook-page showing their amazing delicious ice cream, waffles and fruit, offering the first customer a free ice cream to begin the day!

As gamers and people of esports, we have many ideas and creative thoughts, we know technology, and we can use this combo to help businesses. Is that esports? No, but it is a way to make money, so you can do more activities for your esports organization.

24 ❖ LOCAL MEDIA DEAL

Contact every local media outlet and offer them to do a weekly "Esports News" article for their print and online media. Nearly all of traditional omnibus media outlets know nothing about esports, and your esports column every week will bring new, interesting content to their media which will attract a new target audience (which they need). You can make a deal of one article per week for one year, or more. You can offer to do a podcast, a few videos, or join their sports section, to bring esports to them. The outlet will pay you for great content that will attract and/or engage readers and users.

25 ❖ CUT COSTS

Cutting costs is a great way to build a strong esports organization. Let's say you have a few esports teams, and you need to travel to tournaments and are looking for a partner to cover these costs. Instead of closing a deal with an airline or hotel chain, you can plan the trip, and see if you can negotiate a discount on your travel and accommodation expenses. It would be awesome with a partner to cover all costs, but saving expenses is really important. Having one person dedicated to reduce costs, can for most organizations, be really helpful.

All in all, it is a good idea to look at your plans and list all the expenses for the current and following years, and see how these can be lowered. Usually, costs can be negotiated; all we have to do is try.

Chapter 10

Fundraising

There are a number of different funds that provide subsidies to organizations and to promote, among other things, sporting, and popular cultural initiatives. All approved organizations have the option to apply for various forms of financial support for new activities, projects and equipment purchases. Use Google to find funds and grants at the local, regional, national and international levels, and start applying for the ones that best suit your organization's needs.

LOCAL FUNDRAISING

❯ MUNICIPALITY GRANTS

There are major differences in how and to what extent various municipalities provide support to an organization. Your organization should therefore arrange a meeting with your municipality to gain more information on which pools and subsidy schemes to which your organization can apply. It is important to investigate whether your organization can expect a continuous grant from the municipality or can only apply for grants in the form of lump sums. Some municipalities choose to sponsor organizations through their marketing budget, an opportunity you should consider.

❯ MUNICIPAL GRANT - ORGANIZATION FACILITIES

Some municipalities provide subsidies for an organization's facilities. They may issue grants for the purchase of equipment or grants for remodeling costs among other expenses. Contact your municipality and find out if your organization is able to apply for grants for facilities and how to complete the process.

❯ EXPERIMENTAL AND DEVELOPMENT FUNDS

Some municipalities have an experimental and development pool that issues grants for the development of new initiatives in the municipality and in some cases for the start-up costs of new organizations. Contact your municipality for more information on the various subsidy options for organizations.

> ACTIVITY FUNDS

Some municipalities have so-called activity funds and provide support for the development of new and different activities as well as active participation in cultural and leisure activities. Contact your municipality and learn more about whether your organization can benefit from activity funds.

> MUNICIPAL GRANTS FOR COACHING & MANAGEMENT TRAINING

Approved organizations can sometimes apply for municipal grants for the training of managers and instructors and get reimbursed for expenses related to course activities.

There are several different funds that provide subsidies for organizations and to promote, among other things, sporting, and popular cultural initiatives. All approved organizations have the option to apply for various funds for financial support for new activities, projects and equipment purchases for example.

Although there are many funds to choose from immediately, there are also many applicants and it is difficult to find the right fit. It is therefore important that you and your organization correctly handle the research process and thoroughly prepare before applying.

10 step guide to apply for grants and funds

① START IN TIME

It is important to apply for grants at the proper time. Grants are typically given out annually and generally only support current and future initiatives, not past projects.

Remember that your project must be a non-profit, accessible to many and beneficial to society overall.

② PREPARE YOURSELF THOROUGHLY

Be prepared and describe your organization and its purpose. What idea or vision have you built the organization on? What makes your organization different? What do you want to achieve with organization? Make sure you have a strong message and let your passion for your project shine through.

③ DEVELOP A REALISTIC BUDGET

A transparent and realistic budget is crucial when seeking funds or financial grants. If a fund invests money in your project, both parties need to know exactly where the money goes. Show that any financial subsidy will be used purposefully and with care.

④ FIND STRONG PARTNERS

It is important to have strong partners as they can act as a stamp of quality and approval to the fund. Consider whom you can work with and who can contribute to your project. Is it relevant to involve the municipality, other organizations, schools or companies?

⑤   USE YOUR NETWORK

Map your contacts. Who do you know and how can they help you?
Do you know someone sitting on the board of a fund? Do you know
someone who has experience with fundraising? Do you know someone who understands finances and can help prepare a financial plan?
Use your entire network: old classmates, colleagues, Facebook friends
and parents of your children's friends are a few great examples of
where to look for assistance.

⑥   SELECT RELEVANT FUNDS

Use various databases, manuals and the Internet to find relevant
funds. Search for keywords related to your project. Learn what type
of projects the selected funds have previously provided grants for and
what types of projects and activities they do NOT support. Evaluate
whether your project is within the focus areas of the fund.

⑦   START A DIALOGUE

Are you looking for a fund that has a secretary and/or phone number?
If so, take advantage of it. Call and get answers to your questions. Present your idea and get advice and guidance on your application. Ask in
advance if your project is eligible for the grant before you apply.

⑧   TAILOR YOUR APPLICATION

Do not submit a generic application to all funds. Make sure that at
least 20% of your application is targeted to a specific fund. Target
your application based on the fund's special values and priorities. For
example, find key words and values on the fund's website and use
them in your application if possible. This shows that you have gone
the extra mile and created a unique application for their grant.

⑨   DOUBLE CHECK YOUR APPLICATION

Did you forget anything? Remember that your application must include information about the purpose of the project, activities and supposed results. Include information about your audience and how you want to market the project to the target audience. Remember to include the project budget and financing plan.

⑩   GIVE THANKS AND FOLLOW UP

If a fund chooses to support you project, thank the fund and build the way for further cooperation. Keep the fund up-to-date when you hit milestones and grow, and show how the fund's contribution has made a difference for your esports team. You can also invite representatives from the fund to opening day or other activities. If necessary, send a mid-term evaluation preferably with pictures or video so that the fund can see exactly for what purposes you have used their money.

Chapter 11

Investors

Talking to angel investors and trying to land a seed investment could be the way you want to fund your goals. Based on interviews with IPO Capital and a few other investors, here are the main mistakes esports teams and organizations made when talking to investors that led them to fail.

IPO Capital invest capital as well as provide access to strategic human resources to cash-flow positive Nordic businesses. Their primary focus is on family or founder owned businesses that could benefit from a generational change of ownership whereby they provide an exit strategy to the current shareholders and serve as the new stewards that care for the business and preserve the founder's life's work.

❯ LACK OF SYNERGY IN THE TEAM
Who are you, what have you done, how dedicated is your team, and what will you do together that no one else can?

❯ LACK OF UNIQUE PROFILING AND STORYTELLING
Why is your project unique and how do you differentiate from everyone else doing almost exact the same thing? Why invest in your project?

❯ LACK OF CLEAR BUSINESS PLAN
How do you make money? Where is the business opportunity and how will you grow the business?

❯ LACK OF MEASUREMENT
Which metrics can investors use to measure the investment and the growth of the project?

❯ LACK OF RISK MANAGEMENT
How likely is it that the investor gets their investment back?

> **LACK OF VISION**
Where is your project in 3-5 years?

> **LACK OF TACTICS**
What goals will you achieve in the next 2-3 years?

> **LACK OF OPERATIONS**
How will you reach your goals over the next 1-2 years?

Working closely with an investor could be an idea, but they vary from project to project.

Case Study: Bredballe IF esport

> WHAT IS 'FORENINGSLIV'?

In Denmark, we have a unique history of playing sports together in clubs – we call them foreninger. In our foreninger, we meet in our spare time and play sports as a team or as a community of athletes in individual sports . To participate, one must be a paying member of the club.

In a Danish sports club, you might meet your colleague or neighbor on the track, where he or she coaches your daughter's football team. Your banker might be the chairperson of the local tennis club, and your boss might be serving coffee during a weekend tournament. All these individuals are volunteering in their spare time without being paid. The key concepts in 'foreningsliv' are community, volunteering and room for diversity.

> BREDBALLE IF

Bredballe IF is a local sports association in the city of Vejle, Denmark, offering football, badminton, gymnastics, tennis and esports. The purpose of the association is to gather all those interested in sports and strengthen companionship and create unity between the members of the association.

> THE PURPOSE OF BREDBALLE IF ESPORT

The Bredballe IF esports department was established in May 2018 and in only half a year has created an attractive training environment with 100 paying members, 11 teams and 15 coaches.

The purpose of the department is to create and promote an interest in esports, while creating a framework for the community. This is done by gathering all members under the best possible conditions to practice esports locally. A strong focus and high priority are given to teaching online behavior, strategy planning, collaboration, effective communication and structured training.

The steering committee consists of four managers, with different skill sets and competences in business, esports, finance, marketing, PR, sales, is security and social science.
At Bredballe esport we have our own esports center, in the sports association's clubhouse, with 20 gaming stations serving more than 100 paying members.

Members are primarily boys between 8-17 years from the local city, playing CS:GO and Fortnite on a grassroots and social level. While members pay a subscription to the club, in return they get training, make friends and role models, and participate in healthy activities. They get to be with each other in person, give high fives and have fun with each other and with esports, activities that strengthen participants' people skills and teamwork. As a result, it provides a great benefit to the local club and community.

❯ CREATING BREDBALLE IF ESPORT
- April 2018: The department is approved at Bredballe IF's extraordinary general meeting. Started searching for funds for 6 PCs.
- August 2018: Season 1 - First official training day with 10 PCs.
- Start 2019: Season 2 – Purchase of another 7 PCs (17 PCs in total).
- Summer 2019: Purchase of 3 additional PCs (20 PCs in total).

❯ MEMBERSHIP
- Budget in March 2018: 4 coaches / team x 6 PCs = 24 paying members.
- August 2018: 6 coaches / team x 10 PCs = 60 paying members
- October 2018: 14 coaches, 10 teams, 10 PCs = 80 paying members (+ 22 on waiting list)
- January 2019: 15 coaches, 11 teams, 17 PCs = 100 paying members.

ECONOMY 2018

Expenses

Computers and gear	111,496.34 kr.	14,933.49 €
Software	1,315.68 kr.	176.22 €
Marketing, shirts	17,874.50 kr.	2,394.06 €
Security, keys	3,466.35 kr.	464.27 €
Esport coach education	2,914.85 kr.	390.41 €
Tournement fees	3,200.00 kr.	428.60 €
Miscellaneous	3,708.40 kr.	496.69 €
Total	**143,976.12 kr.**	**19,283.74 €**

Revenue

Partners, grants and funds	125.166,00 kr.	16,764.36 €
Subscription, paying members	26.857,00 kr.	3,597.15 €
Total	**152.023,00 kr.**	**20,361.51 €**

PARTNERS

Revenue comes from several sources. The first mistake we made was to send the same copy / pasted email to all potential partners. We learned that it made the most sense to talk directly to local partners and businesses, as well as regional and national businesses, to tell them our story, about the difference we are making for the community and the young people we have as members.

Our work focused on offering a partner's logo on a gaming chair in our esports center, or simply asking them to sponsor one or more gaming stations.

We offer partners a range of activities for them to engage with our club, such as: tournaments, logos on our website, social media and clothing.

We also provide multiple opportunities for partner activations in our esport center. We create unique content, pictures, videos and articles which create reach and engagement with our partners throughout our various media channels. We go to events with our partners, creating activities, training sessions and matches in stores or at larger events, which promotes a positive image for our partners.

❯ FUNDS AND GRANTS
We use Google and search for local, regional or national grants and funds. The work we do in our esports club benefits our members in many ways. Our members experience growth and development in their health and social lives. Our club also helps young people engage in the local community, become part of a team, make friends, do volunteer work, become healthier and better at esports.

We help young people develop as humans, get an education and strengthen their relations with their family and friends. These are benefits and outcomes that many funds and grants will support.

Bredballe IF esport was formed in April 2018, where we started from the ground up. As of spring 2019, we have our own esports center with 20 gaming stations, 15 coaches and more than 100 paying members. Our goal is to gradually expand our activities to accommodate 40 gaming stations and 250 members.

To learn more about Bredballe IF, please contact Jesper at: jesper@ hyldenbrandt.com

Chapter 13

Inspiration from the esports industry: Razer

TOBIAS WESTFALL BRØNDUM COMMUNITY
& ESPORTS SPECIALIST WITH RAZER (EUROPE).

I had several talks with Tobias, and here are some of his best ideas on how esport teams and organizations can work successfully with partners.

When reaching out to potential partners, build a strong marketing deck that will explain who you are, what you do, how you can work with partners and where the business opportunity is.

❯ WHO ARE YOU?
Describe who you are in the leadership team, what you have done and why you are unique. How is the team composed? Have you worked with each other before? How high is the probability of success with your esport team or organization?

❯ SHOW YOUR DETAILS
Show the management team, but also the esports players and team. Show figures on social media reach, streaming reach and online reach, to help potential partners understand how far you can carry their brand and messages. Show opportunity to grow, it is great that you have a good reach on social media for example, but what are your plans for growth the next 1, 2, 3 years?

❯ WHAT DO YOU HAVE TO OFFER?
Be very specific about which services your organization can provide to the partner. Logo placements, events, naming teams/activities. Streaming layovers, creative content creation, visibility on streams,

social media and web – and so on. Be creative and intelligent with your packaging so potential partners easily understands the idea and understand how far you can take their brand and how easy it is for you to do so.

❯ WHAT IS IN IT FOR THE PARTNER?
This is important to understand. You have to make sure that you understand the goals and visions of your partners. If your partner is looking for huge reach, you need to focus on that but if the partner is looking for activation or creative content creation, you need to focus on that. Therefore, it is very important to clear out expectations before signing the contract. When you understand where your partner wants to go, and where you can go together, you can get to work and plan, and execute.

❯ LOOKING AWESOME!
Always use high quality pictures and video. Underestimated, maybe, but make sure that you use quality pictures and video content when you are talking to a partner. If you use poor quality pictures or video, the partner might think that you will put their brand into a poor-quality context as well.

❯ WHAT ARE YOU DOING RIGHT NOW?
Show how you are activating followers via social media and streams, right now. How do you interact, how do you do events, and how do you talk to and activate your fans and followers?
Show how you are creating creative content, right now. Potential partners want to feel safe, working with you, and it helps them feel safe when you show them that you know what you are doing. Make sure that the content you produce, follows the partner's marketing rules/guidelines.

❯ TARGET AUDIENCE
A few words on your target audiences. Understand that most partners are looking at markets: countries, languages, and target audiences. When you can be specific and show that your esport organization

penetrates 66% of the US market, it will be easier for you to work with brands that wants to enter, or be present in the US market.

❯ PARTNERS ARE USUALLY LOOKING FOR:
- Reach: get their brand to as many (relevant) people, as possible.
- Brand Awareness: looking to become better known by the right people, to whom they will buy and speak well about their products.
- Quality: be part of esport teams and organizations, who promote quality in every category. (Values, Management, Players, Results, Marketing and Customer/Fan relations).
- Making a difference: Depending on the partner, most campaign managers or marketing executives are looking to make a difference. Either for their company, for themselves or for the team they are working with. If you can understand their inner motivation for what they do, you can help them be successful, and that will make them like you and prioritize your esports team or organization.

Razer™ is the world's leading lifestyle brand for gamers. The triple-headed snake trademark of Razer is one of the most recognized logos in the global gaming and esports communities. With a fan base that spans every continent, the company has designed and built the world's largest gamer-focused ecosystem of hardware, software and services.

Chapter 14

Inspiration from the esports industry: Red Bull

INSIGHTS AND ADVICE FROM TALKS WITH ANDREAS BJERRUM LARSEN & KASPER KJEMPFF, RED BULL DENMARK.

"8 pointers to consider before contacting a potential partner"
– from my talks with Andreas and Kasper at Red Bull Denmark.

1 Who are you and why are you unique?

Describe who you are as a human being, what are you passionate about, what is your inner motivation and explain why you, your esports team or organization is unique. What do you do that no one else is doing (compared to all the other 400 million English-speaking gamers in the world)?

2 Who is your management?

Describe who your team / management is – what is their passion? What have they achieved before? Why are they unique and how are you strong together? How do you supplement each other?

3 What is your vision?

Describe what your vision is. Which journey do you want the potential partner to be a part of? What are your dreams and where do you want to go and why?

4 What goals do you have?

Describe what goals you have. How will you work with your vision to achieve your goals?

5 What do you do?

Describe what you have invested in the team, organization and yourself. What have you done so far, to achieve your visions and goals (time, money and resources)?

6 What are others doing?

Describe what others have invested in the team, organization and yourself. What have other people or partners done so far to achieve your visions and goals (time, money and resources)?

7 Why are you writing to Red Bull?

Explain why you write to Red Bull as a potential partner (rather than other brands).

8 How do you think Red Bull can contribute?

Describe how you think Red Bull can join your journey and together, create a meaningful partnership for both you and Red Bull.

The S-11 model

S FOR SUCCES!

Use this model. It is a contraction of all the advice and experiences I have gained over the last 20 years.

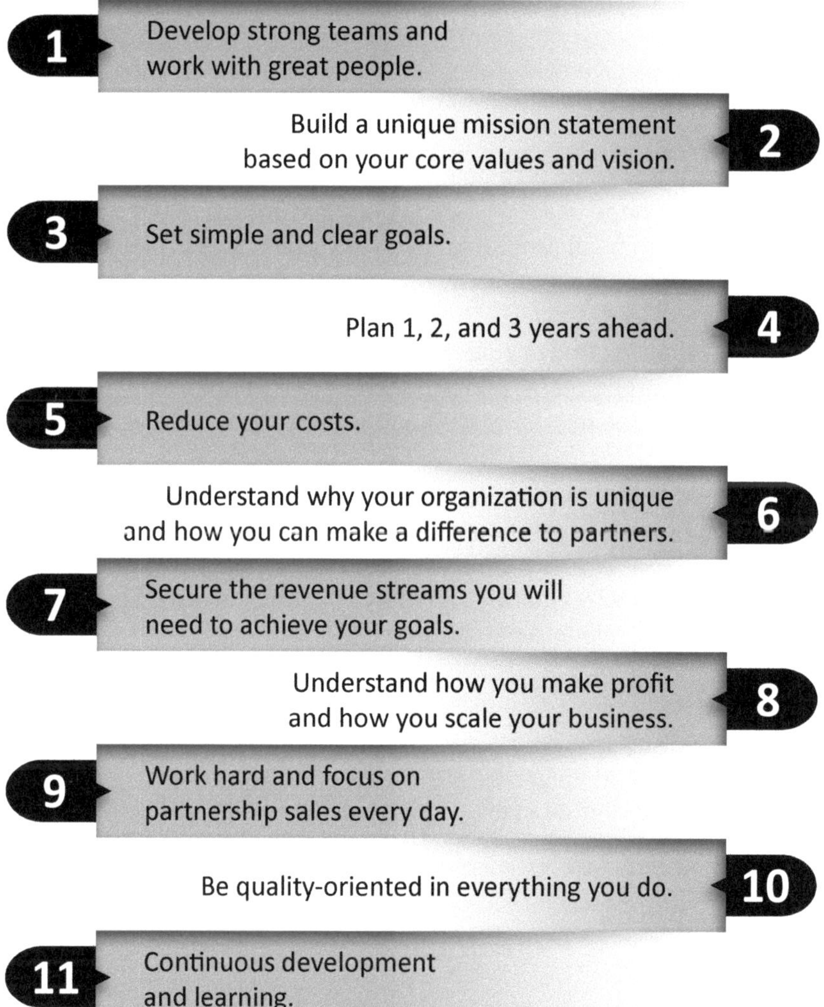

Outro

Back to the beginning.

Building an esports organization or team is hard. It is hard to find the right people, hard to find the players and coaches, hard to find a location (if needed), and hard to define an organization that differentiates itself from everyone else. You have to build a brand, social media strategy, and manage everything - and on top of it all - create revenue to make everything run smoothly. None of these are easy tasks.

My goal with this guide is to help you with your esports organization, club or team. I hope I have inspired you to think outside the box so you can begin to build profitable revenue streams and achieve your esports dreams, just like so many others.

1. Key takeaways in this guide:
2. Develop strong teams and work with great people.
3. Build a unique mission statement based on your core values and vision.
4. Set simple and clear goals.
5. Plan 1, 2, and 3 years ahead.
6. Reduce your costs.
7. Understand why your organization is unique and how you can make a difference to partners
8. Secure the revenue streams you will need to achieve your goals.
9. Understand how you make profit and how you scale your business.
10. Work hard and focus on partnership sales every day.
11. Be quality-oriented in everything you do.
12. Continuous development and learning.

All the best wishes,

Martin Fritzen